CHRISTMAS EVE
at the
EPSOM CIRCLE McDONALD'S
and Other Poems

MAREN C. TIRABASSI

CONTENTS

Christmas comes   1

Introduction   3

MEMORIES OF THE SEASON

Tale as old as time ...   7

Christmas Eve at the Epsom Circle McDonald's   8

Wasn't That a Mighty Day?   11

Before the rehearsal   12

Holiday Visit   13

Snow? *(writing prompt in the correctional facility, Bridgewater, Massachusetts)*   14

Getting the tree   16

Trimming the tree   18

Blue Christmas   19

Trains   21

Opening the window   23

His fingers remember   25

Economies of Winter   27

Pageant   28

SOME DAYS HOLD OUR MEMORIES...

World AIDS Day (December 1) *Improv on Psalm 137:1-6*   33

Feast of our Lady of Guadalupe (December 12)   35

A Prayer for December 14   37

REFLECTIONS ON THE PANDEMIC FOR ADVENT AND CHRISTMAS

In a long year of Advent   41

A pandemic pageant   42

Narnia   44

Christmas greetings to all the closed inns   45

Mask on the red-nosed reindeer   46

The Work of Advent *(After Howard Thurman)*   47

Where will we find our "Silent Night"   49

A sleighful of "santas"   50

Miracles   51

POEMS FROM CHARLES DICKENS' A CHRISTMAS CAROL

Ebenezer Scrooge is warned by Jacob Marley   55

The Ghost of Christmas Past shows Scrooge himself,
an unloved, unwanted child 56

Scrooge is shown a Christmas party thrown by his first employer Fezziwig 57

Scrooge is reminded of choosing business success over love 58

The Ghost of Christmas Past leaves Scrooge 59

Ebenezer is taken by the Ghost of Christmas Present to witness the
unexpectedly happy Christmas of people Scrooge considers unfortunate. 60

Scrooge observes the Christmas Day celebration of his nephew Fred
whose invitation he turned down as a waste of time 61

Scrooge is shown two hidden children, Want and Ignorance.
"Beware them," says Christmas, "beware Ignorance the most." 62

The Ghost of Christmas Yet to Come shows Scrooge the death
of Tiny Tim, possible if there is no intervention 63

Scrooge is shown a pawn shop selling the sheets and curtains
of his bed and his clothes 64

The Ghost of Christmas Yet to Come offers
another chance to ... curmudgeons 65

The best-known line in "A Christmas Carol" is spoken by Tiny Tim 67

"He went to church and walked about the streets and watched the
people hurrying to and fro ... and found he took pleasure in it all."
A Christmas Carol 68

SOME POEMS FROM TRADITIONS ... OLD OR NEWER

A Conversation about Her 71

Las Posadas 73

Mistletoe 74

Fields and floods, rocks, hills and plains ... 75

Magnificat 77

Lighting the Dark 79

The Johannine Nativity 80

Improv on Dr. Seuss' The Grinch who Stole Christmas 82

THE LONG O OF ADVENT

O parable-maker, Christ 87

O antiphon for those who wait 88

O antiphon for those who suffer sexual violence 89

O antiphon for Advent in the Pandemic 90

O antiphon for the Festival of St. Nicholas*(December 6 or December 19)* 92

O antiphon for those in recovery 93

O antiphon for all the beasts 95

O antiphon for the winter solstice 96

O Tannenbaum 98

O antiphon for Christmas Eve 99

PRAYERS FROM SONGS OF THE SEASON

"Little Drummer Boy," 103

"Do You Hear what I Hear?" 104

"Hard Candy Christmas," 105

"I wonder as I wander" 107

"Go Tell It on the Mountain" 109

AND IT COMES...

'Twas the (ordinary) Cold Before Christmas 113

God, I didn't get it all done 115

FOR TWELVE DAYS

Mourning after, Tamir Rice 119

Shall yourselves find blessing 120

Tinsel 122

New Year's Eve Morning 124

A New Year and a Small Cow 125

Epiphany, the story comes again… 126

epiphany story 128

According to Matthew 129

I'll keep it there 130

AND WHAT COMES NEXT...

For this Time Being *(After W.H. Auden)* 135

About the Author 137

Christmas comes

Christmas comes to my friend in withdrawal
at Strafford County House of Correction,
and the ninety-year-old grandpa
in the nursing home
who hasn't spoken in six months.

It comes to the beagle who bays at the skunk,
balsams and frasiers leaning wrapped
against the fence in the Christmas tree lot,
and many children who also,
for some reason, and in some place,
have not been chosen.

Christmas comes to the shoppers who pause
to listen to the bell-ringing
and put a little money in the kettle.
It comes even if they do it
because someone is watching,
and it comes for those who never stop.

Christmas comes to the man
who mourns his partner,
and to the woman who mourns her mother,

and Christmas comes to partner and mother –
differently, of course –
less fruitcake, more angels.

Christmas comes in December
to unprepared pageant committees
and the soldier deployed.
It comes to small dancers in the Nutcracker
and to a previously unemployed man
who grows and powders a beard

1

because mall Santas
earn more with their own facial hair.

Christmas comes in 2020
to the grieving and the exhausted,
those who have never known
so much loneliness
or so much desperation just to be alone,
those facing financial disaster
or deciding to never nurse again.

Christmas comes whether we are ready or not;
it comes whether we want it or not;
it comes whether we used to believe,
or try to believe, or are afraid to believe.

Christmas comes with presents and with absence.
It comes as expected,
and it comes as a nearly unbearable surprise.

Introduction

Joy to the world –
a descending scale, played with love.

That's what the carol of that name is. I didn't know it. Eight falling notes, in order. The difference between an exercise for piano students and music that stirs my heart is placing pauses. This is a book of poetry for Advent and Christmas and the tail end of the star we call Epiphany. Some of these poems are a few years old, like the title poem, which is a memory I revisit every December 24th, and some are very new, but every year for every one of us the pauses come in different places.

This season celebrates the gift of God. In the Incarnation, God chose human life – acne and agony, clueless friends as well as the kiss of betrayal, the real possibility of dying as an infant or being scammed by the Tempter in the wilderness and ultimate vulnerability for One who flung the Aurora Borealis.

I have written books of liturgy for church services in my ministry. These poems, in contrast, are very personal reflections and the stories they tell come from my life and observations. Join me putting wooden trains around the tree, hearing Magnificat as wrapped in a tilma full of roses portrayed in a snow globe, tasting the truth that "blue" Christmas can be baked into cookies, tying a mask on the red-nosed reindeer, and being changed by "Wasn't That a Mighty Day?" sung in Langston Hughes' "Black Nativity."

When we come to this Advent, we will not be the same people we were last year. Some of us will have greeted new children born and many, many of us will have grieved since last Epiphany. Christmas will come anyway. Perhaps we will be disoriented like people of that long ago census or the camel-sore magi than we have been in a long time.

Probably without so much traveling.

Maren C. Tirabassi
August, 2020

Memories of
the Season

Tale as old as time ...

The little girl who was the Bethlehem star
in our Christmas pageant –
who led the magi on their wandering,
bright in her Belle dress
from Beauty and the Beast,
and then was held high by her mother
over the manger where the Christ-child lay –
has been deported.

Ah, there are so many modern Herods,
and a rareness in the traveling of wisdoms.

Journey well, Ana, and please remember –
wherever your mother holds you,
there the Christ child is.

Christmas Eve at the
Epsom Circle McDonald's

The kids with the santa hats
are selling hamburgers
more cheerfully
because they feel the season
and are glad for early closing.
A boyfriend comes in
and hangs over the counter
pressing against tattered garland
looped to the finger level
of children.

A family with three toddlers,
jazzy with excitement,
are traveling to Maine
in the drizzle of the holy evening.
The littlest boy
in red and green plaid Oshkosh
runs in circles,
strangling French fries in his hand.
Tired of the car and
already eager for presents and bed,
his little sneakers tramp
like angel feet.

An older couple in a corner
talk quietly about their daughter
who's been dead
four Christmases now.
They could have gone
to their son-in-law's house.
His kind new wife
invited them with her family,

but it didn't seem right.
And this was the very
brightest place – it
looked like a star
when they drove down
the highway,
and they knew there would be
children.

A divorced Dad with
Budweiser on a black T-shirt
jokes with his
six year old daughter
over milk shakes.
A clumsily wrapped present
perches on the
molded plastic seat.
He is trying to make
the very best treat he can
of their Christmas hour
before bringing her
back to her Mom's house.
Brown eyes shine at him
and he thinks
she is excited for later –
for Santa and all –
but she's looking at him
all over
memorizing the gift.

The preacher
is on her way to church
to remember Bethlehem
out loud
for the folks who come
to break bread and
light little candles

with paper circles on them
that keep the wax
from dripping on their hands
as they sing "Silent Night."

Most of them
have heard the story
about the child before,
and so has she.
She has come here first,
just to sit for a while
and watch the
christmas eve communion.

Wasn't That a Mighty Day?

I am watching what was called
"Wasn't that a Mighty Day?"
by Langston Hughes,
but for a long time
has been known as "Black Nativity."

At Tremont Temple in Boston
the soloist is belting out –
"There is no room at the hotel!"
and we are all feeling cold.

Then Mary gives birth
with the rhythm of African drums,
and of all women who birth babies.

It's not as universal as cold,
but many of us remember that pain,
though we cannot imagine
the pain that is yet to come
in raising this child,

in raising so many children.

The magi are not performers
but they are honored Black people
from the city of Boston.

None of them sing or dance
but are chosen because of their gifts.
It ends with a child's soliloquy
spoken straight to me,
just me,
like it is for me,
and even for those whose imagination
didn't take them to pain or cold,

to make this mighty day real.

Before the rehearsal

A five year old says her sister is "pageant."

I know she means pregnant,
but her frame of reference
for unwed mother
is leading lady in the Bethlehem story.

She needs me to share how happy she is,
a little afraid, confused
and I am, too, thinking of others
pregnant today –
deliriously happy, scared to death,
or somewhere in-between.

And that this, too, is true –
all of us in some way in this season,
are "pageant" with God.

Holiday Visit

She is old, sitting on a bench
outside the memory care unit,
where she has come to visit a friend.

She watches children
from the preschool next door
play in new fallen snow.

She laughs at her cranky knees
which could never replicate those antics.

She holds out a black gloved hand
to catch the flakes,
then opens her fingers wide
making her own perfect snow angel.

Snow?

(writing prompt in the correctional
facility, Bridgewater, Massachusetts)

Well, it didn't snow much
in Philadelphia, not on Delancey Street,

but he remembers one year,
one December it was,
when his Mama told him
to run fast and get his sled
before the wet snow melted off the street.
She made his sisters
get off their butts and watch him,
which they were not happy to do.

But, oh, how the wind blew
in his face, and
he almost went right under a car.
Later he warmed his hands
above the burner on the stove
and drank hot chocolate.

Only one other time – he was walking
with his girlfriend Angel
home from school.
He was a teenager then,
but it was before he started
getting into trouble.
They were real sweet –
nothing more, because Mama was strict.

It was the last day
before winter vacation,
and the snow started coming down,
slush-messy on the pavement,

14

but on Angel's black hair
it was white stars and pretty,
just like his Grandmama's tatting
on the back of a sofa.
He was planning to tell Angel
he loved her, but, like he said,
she was just so sweet,

and he didn't want to spoil
all that sweetness
with his bad-assed self.

But now he wishes
he had said something to her,
something about how good
and warm he felt
when he looked at her,
like the Jersey shore even in winter,
something crazy like that,
or maybe how he wanted
to be good for her.
But that was the night
Angel and her four brothers
were killed in the big fire
that took down a whole block of
Delancey Street projects.

And that's how he remembers
snow —
all light and sparkling
on a girl's black hair,
like she was frosted pretty
for Christmas,

that, and sledding, too,
and just how fast a little boy
can go downhill.

Getting the tree

The young man picks me up
and we go to find a Christmas tree,
knowing I need it today
to brighten the gloomy weather.

He walks the lot, every row,
shaking one and then another –
Balsam, Frasier,
shorter, taller, fuller, thinner –
tamping each trunk
hard against the ground
until the green is shaken down

and shows what branch and needle
will look like
when it is decorated
with memories of a lifetime.

This one. It is the perfect tree –
it will smell
like winter come inside,
for the old parents
and the curious beagle
who will be bound to sneeze.

He laughs as men always do
to make a moment of camaraderie
around the heater
as they cut the trunk.
These city guys working for a charity
rub their hands, puff to see their breath
like they are building a cabin
years and years ago.

I go to find wreaths
and leave them to their small rite.

When I return, he's swaddled the tree
keeping branches straight,
squeezed it in the back of the car.

He turns to me and smiles.
He could have cut one in the woods,
but this is better,
it's how he goes to church.

Trimming the tree

The woman trims the Christmas tree.
She is ninety-six,
and I can remember a Christmas,
maybe twenty-years ago,
when she was too depressed
to answer the doorbell
and left her family on the steps

Now she stands,
one hand to the walker,
and the other to a glass ornament –
fragile as a human life.

She finds the perfect place,
where it hangs
free of the dark green branches,
and now it shines
in a string of holiday light.

Blue Christmas

No laundry tonight,
no bill-paying, phone calls, texts –
I'm baking.

There are chocolate-mint pinwheels,
anginetti, snickerdoodles,
molasses cookies, macaroons
(with red and green cherries),
shortbread, anise drops,
almond crescents, snowballs,
GF peanut butter blossoms
with vegan kisses,

also sugar cookies cut
as trees or bells with icing,
sprinkles, or crushed candy cane,
and, don't forget,
gender-inclusive gingerbread.

My best friend and I
always made our cookies together
on a mom, then senior sleepover,
pulling pans out of the oven
till after midnight,
then playing a quick game
of Boggle to cool off.

It is different for everyone,
a joy remembered
in some quite ordinary
crumb of the holy season,

but whenever blue Christmas
arrives for anyone of us
God's there,
apron on, flour to the elbows
in our lives,
sharing our taste of tears.
(for Diane Beaudoin Karr, not ever forgotten)

Trains

The wooden train arrives
by FedEx
before seven in the morning,
and the dog wakes barking
at the delivery
as if trying to catch
some caboose of his dream.

With its black engine,
red cars, smooth brown tracks
it will travel by hand
around the Christmas tree
ready to greet my grandsons,
still too small for
the electric trains in the attic.

I remember
the stories my father told
about a job he had when he was ten
in Prairie Hill, Missouri,
getting up every night to run
from his Dad's general store
to the railway hotel
and wake the conductor
and the engineer
for the three AM freight.

He was not to leave
till he saw them in their boots.

We put trains
in the hands of small boys –

some responsibility,
some really great loud noises,
a few stories of the past,
and dreams
of many places to go.

Opening the window

The woman cannot go out often
because she is caring for her husband,
and she hates to ask folks
to stay with him
when it's not a doctor's visit
or grocery shopping.

December is full of events
she loved to attend in years past –
choral concerts,
plays at the elementary school
where she used to teach,
elaborate gingerbread creations
at the museum,
caroling in the nursing home,
well, even shopping –

she has missed them all,
but most of all, Christmas Eve.

She used to go to both services –
the children's live nativity
and the choir's carols and lessons,
but not this year.

People are with their own families –
she would hardly want to ask
them to come here,
and then, again,
she wouldn't want to leave him.

But after he's in bed,
she goes upstairs to open the window
and let in the frosty night air

to cool everything down,
and just then bells begin to ring.

It's not her own church,
in fact, she not sure what church
is upwind of her.
She stands in the dark room
looking at a few stars
briefly glimpsed
as the snow clouds gather,

and Christmas comes to her.

His fingers remember

It's a scroogy little half-coal holiday party,
(several weeks late because of snow)
in the memory care unit.
The real present
is that rent will stay the same in the New Year.

But all the same, the egg sandwiches,
cheese and crackers, meat balls, chocolate cake,
look tired, resentful,
under the tattered decorations,
and the staff are in grays and blues
beginning to look *not* a lot like Christmas.

Many of the residents, without family
and not really understanding
this is meant to be special for them,
because no one has bothered to unwrap
the sweetest present, memory,
the way the tight ribbon
needs to be untied again and again,
have gone conveniently off to bed early
leaving empty tables cluttered with dishes.

Then the man who was a church organist
and worked in nightclubs, too,
for more than forty years
is coaxed to the old upright piano.

He insists he no longer can play,
but, when his fingers touch the keys,
black and white with carols hidden inside,
his face changes, turns Rudolf bright,

and we shut our eyes
as he leads us
to a concert hall and a jazz club,
several sanctuaries, a ballroom, Bethlehem.

Economies of Winter

She stands in a puddle of snowmelt,
with damp strands of blond hair
pasted across her forehead.
Her fingers in the pocket
of her Goodwill coat
rustle cigarette cellophane.

She asks for a Christmas for her kids.
It's a strange expression,
but I know what she means.
She names girls of twelve, ten,
and a boy of seven.

My office in the congregational church
is warm and new
and I sit in a glider chair
bought with my holiday bonus.
Toying with her,
I ask what's on the children's list
like I'm some kind of self-important
north pole detective.

She wants money,
and she has practiced grateful
in the mirror
many times this morning.

She knows one thing –
people are generous when it's kids.

I know two things –
she already has presents
from the Pittsfield Roman Catholics,
and she is playing the system
just to stay even.

If it were a game, I'd be ahead.

Pageant

The littlest children were supposed to be sheep,
being watched in the fields by night,
and their mothers sent them
in black pants and
white sweatshirts inscribed "BAA."

A church lady stayed up all night
sewing construction paper lamb-ears
to cellophane headbands,
but there was a narthex revolt
and the kindergarten shepherds
(whose crooks had been confiscated
because of fighting),
tripping over their fathers' bathrobes,
hitched up over their fathers' neckties,
lost moral authority of their flock
and the nursery kids insisted
on wearing their ears – not
droopy-down, but straight up

and suddenly there appeared
over the Judean hills –
a multitude of bunny rabbits.

And the one giggle that started
in the third grade angel choir
among small girls shiny with braces
and tinsel in their hair, and
spread through the more mature
eastern caravan with their vinegar bottles,
jewelry boxes and tinfoil crowns,

until it reached even the principals –
the pillow-fattened innkeeper,
Miriam of Nazareth, strained and stiff

with her baby sister in her arms,
Yosef (chosen as accessory because
he is tall and well-behaved)
both parts of the articulated cow,
Gabriel, Prince of Angels,
several of Herod's centurions
with trash can lid shields,

and a young lady with a new lip ring
and green sparkling nails,
crouching behind the pulpit
with a microphone
to be the voice of god.

and just like two-thousand years ago
in the days of Caesar Augustus,
when Quirinius was governor of Syria ...
God laughed!

Some days hold our memories...

World AIDS Day
(December 1)
Improv on Psalm 137:1-6

By the rivers of Boston –
Mystic and Charles –
every year I sit down and cry,
remembering so many
theatre friends
from the seventies in New York.

And on this day
I write a playbill of their names
and their favorite parts.
I sing rainbows
and watch the hanging of quilts.

And I weep by every river,
in Sub-Saharan Africa, Eastern Europe,
Asia, Latin America,
by every willow where HIV /AIDS
has taken the creative ones among us,
many queer
chased away from faith,
and many women the age of girls.

If I forget you, AIDS pandemic,
orphan-maker,
in the midst of other sorrows
let my heart wither,
let my COVID-hope songs
fall silent on the balconies
and in the Zoom boxes of the earth.

If I do not remember
not just to mask, but to ask –
who is testing for this old killer,

then come remind me,
first holy day in Advent,
when every year we cry our names
that we insist that all the world
should be enrolled.

Feast of our Lady of Guadalupe
(December 12)

She was given to me
in a snow globe with an electric cord
to light the shaking
of white fluff and gold sparkle.

Forgive me, I thought she was tacky,
this Mary who also can appear
in a tattoo,
painted on a beer can, a road sign,
a church wall, an alley wall
or a motorcycle leather jacket.

Guadalupe –
happy to be Hailed anywhere
by anyone, even me.

This Mary is mestiza
and all goddess,
where I do not expect to meet either one.
Her mouth, full of Nahuatl words,
magnificats in anyone's language,
and because so many people
have too many religious words
stuffed down them,

(for which, she tells me
I am somewhat responsible)

she comes just to be seen
in color,
turquoise, inked with the stars,
and a full-body halo.

I do not think I'm dreaming.
She asks me to plug her in
and shake her up
because in every generation,
she has roses to give away.

A Prayer for December 14

God, we pray peace in mind
and hope in heart
for brothers. sisters and classmates
of the children who died
at Sandy Hook Elementary School
and in hundreds of school shootings
since that December day.

A Clara is missing the Nutcracker.
A child won't pick chocolates
from the Advent calendar.
A teen is not lit by a disco ball
at the winter formal,
and a college student
is not cramming for finals.

We pray for their friends.

We pray for young people,
afraid of guns or loud noises
or strangers or friends,
home schooled because of fear.

We pray for some who hurt,
whose need for help and attention
is going unnoticed
right now,
and who are growing fascinated
by guns and their power.

We pray for those with access to guns,
for kids who want toy guns
this Christmas –
dreaming of play adventures
when, at the end,
everyone stands up and goes home.

And we also pray,
for those with responsibility
we should be sharing –
teachers, administrators,
school therapists, first responders,
lawmakers and parents –
on this unhappy anniversary.

Reflections on the Pandemic for Advent and Christmas

In a long year of Advent

In a long, long year of Advent,
there has been real waiting,
not the ritual lighting of four candles,

but the month-after-month experience
of living daily hope,
cherishing moments of peace,

claiming joy in masked walks,
drive-by graduations,
car parade birthdays,
curbside commerce, virtual church,
zoomy, skypey, facetimey family,

and grieving losses as deep love
learns to bend
familiar memorial forms.

Much of this year has unfolded
in ways that turn us heartside out –

and now we don't just read this story
in its gathered cultural nostalgia,
but understand more,
about the unexpected pregnancy
of life itself,
the grueling essential work
of watching sheep sleep,

and the foolishness
of wandering somewhere new
in a strange landscape
with the uneasy guidance of a star.

A pandemic pageant

Magi probably wished
for an excuse to put a mask on the camel.
They spit!

All the children in the pageant,
having learned about aerosol particles,
cover sneezes,
stay away from crowds,
and avoid singing.

This is the year we tell them
to listen deeply
and play their own parts
in their own homes,
which will be put together later
by the Tech-angel Gabriel
so that all the world
can livestream Bethlehem.

Small gifts of detail, dialogue,
and imagination,
is the way we learned this story
the first time around.

We accept their suggestion
to mask the camel staying in the church
played by the pastor,
and even give it a line,
"Go on the journey, follow the star,
but take a safe way home."

Then we measure out in spiritual distance
multitudes of heavenly host,
(seeing the shuttle launch helps).
Of course, angels sang, but from the sky!

And we are encouraging everyone
to sing out the window
or into a YouTube a carol or cantata
that does not exist without all its parts,
vocal, ukulele, one cello,
one electric guitar,
one dog contributing a quickly stifled bark,
grandma with maracas.

And all of us to ponder in our hearts.

Narnia

As World War II was beginning, children were evacuated from urban areas in England for fear of Nazi attacks. Three school-aged girls came to live at CS Lewis' home near Oxford. He began the story called, "The Lion, the Witch and the Wardrobe."

There come years when imagination
tells a story about how terrible
it would be,
to have only winter with no Christmas,

though in other years that premise is labeled
"only" children's fiction,
and adults, being who they are,
think it is unreal
or unworthy of true concern.

The second world war was such a time
for stories about
dark winter without hope,
random people turned to solid ice,
a desire for turkish delight,
or whatever candy-selfishness of the time
makes betrayal
of the needs of others acceptable.

Lamp posts show the way,
kindness matters,
even from those who've failed before.
God appears in unexpected ways,
and courage
sometimes needs a horn,
sometimes a drop of healing.

This year may be another time
for just these stories.

Christmas greetings to all the closed inns

Christmas Greetings for all those whose
"inns" have closed this year –

restaurants and book stores,
boutiques and bike shops,
hairdressers and small gyms,
fish markets and franchises,
bodegas and body-shops,
and so many others.

We pray for good memories,
the gratitude of former customers,
the courage of new beginnings,

and the realization
that each innkeeper may never know
how their small business
may have been for someone
a manger-place full of starlight.

Mask on the
red-nosed reindeer

Mask on the red-nosed reindeer,
gloves on the packing elves,
fewer the presents this year –
making happy gifts ourselves.

All of the former christmas'
used to boast of food and toys.
More isn't always better;
loving doesn't come with noise.

2020 Christmas Eve
leads us all to say –
"Anyone with heart on right,
guide us to the true starlight."

Then on a Christmas morning,
wrapped and bowed in simple fun –
Rudolph the Red-Nosed Reindeer
can be found in anyone.

The Work of Advent

(After Howard Thurman)

When the carols of choirs are stilled,

when so many dear ones are gone
it seems like the stars
have blinked their tears into darkness,

when the year has kept so many home
and endangered the homes
of so many others,

when the shepherds of the year
are health care workers,
and, like those flock-keepers long ago,
essential but poorly-honored workers,

the work of Advent begins:

to find the grieving, the fearful, the lost,

to heal those broken in spirit
with the story of an unexpected hope
in another time of great danger,

to feed, clothe, shelter, employ,
those financially insecure,

to release the prisoner –
especially those
in immigration detention,

to rebuild all the nations,
because the epiphany is
that gifts come
not out of our own chimneys
but from strangers who live far away,

to become stable-makers that shelter
peace, health, wisdom
and care for the earth itself,

to sing the carols in our homes
and teach the words and maybe one tune
to someone, perhaps a child,
who longs for a new harmony.

Where will we find our "Silent Night"

In the story behind the carol
we sing while lighting little candles,

it was Christmas Eve and Joseph Mohr,
pastor at St. Nicholas,
gave lyrics to Franz Gruber,
grade school teacher and musician,
and asked for music
that could be played on a guitar
because they could not use the organ.
(Diagnoses vary from flood-damage
to the nibbling of mice.)

All this year of coronavirus
we have been finding new ways
to tell a story we know is true –
picking on a guitar
what cannot resonate in organ chords.

Yet it was the organ mender,
Karl Mauracher,
who took the new carol down the mountain
to share with the whole world.

We, too, will blend
old traditions and new gifts.

In spite of silent nights, Silent Night,
is a song of the heart
undaunted by flood, mice or virus.

A sleighful of "santas"

It's been a year sleighful
of santas and Nicks,
also La Befana, Ded Moroz
(that's Grandfather Frost
with his granddaughter Snegurochka),
Yule Lads, (thirteen, they look like dwarves),
Jultomten (definitely a gnome),
Kris Kringle y Los Reyes Magos –

the ones who deliver the toys
and food, and, in fact,
all the things the heart desires.

Now is the moment to appreciate
the many-named and yet anonymous
deliverers in our time –
employees of the Post Office
and FedEx, UPS, Amazon Prime,
Door Dash, Uber Eats,

the driver of a predawn newspaper,
florists, stores of every kind
and restaurants, too, who deliver,
the neighbor with groceries,
even a dog walker
with a leash-full of canine joy.

This year we certainly know
there can never be
enough carrots, cookies, and milk.

Miracles

A baby is born in a stable.
Toys come from the north pole.
Sometimes angels arrive
when we are awake,
and sometimes in our dreams.

In the beginning was the Word,
older than fear, older than the virus,
and the Word was with God.

We can't define the miracles,
but we put them in new carols –
and then we hum them behind masks,
so that it is safe
for all the children of God.

Poems from Charles Dickens' A Christmas Carol

This sequence of poems is a contemporary reflection on the well-shared ghost story of the season.

Ebenezer Scrooge is warned
by Jacob Marley

I'm grateful for jacob marleys,
people who warn me
by sharing their tough times and mistakes.

Many sit in church basements
in a circle of chairs, reciting twelve steps,
living twelve traditions.

Others are therapists,
parole officers, teachers,

friends who damaged a relationship
with partner, parent, child –
and say to me –
don't let your anger go deep and old,

or colleagues who lived for work
and missed fishing, dancing,
hanging even one ornament on a tree.

I'm grateful to jacob marleys,
dragging their clanking remorse
through my heart,
painting their faces on my door knocker
till I notice that I can shape
something new
from the bad dreams in my life.

The Ghost of Christmas Past shows Scrooge himself, an unloved, unwanted child

The world is full of children
unwanted, unloved,
little cared for –
as infants, youngsters or teens.

Some are abused, suffer incest,
are shuffled
from place to place, bullied,
unfriended or not-accepted
in a newly blended family, new school,
in a sports team or a drama club.
Some are isolated
as transgender, on the spectrum,
too poor, cognitive disability,
juvie record or hungry.

We find them in mirrors,
on days when we need to open windows.

Scrooge is shown a Christmas party thrown by his first employer Fezziwig

God, who is a notorious lover of parties,
great food, comet-bright decorations,
and that flash mob of angels,

puts fezziwigs in my path,
and I have slowly learned to be generous,
and even more slowly to stop working
all the time, all the time,
to eat, drink and laugh,
to get over myself and dance
even when I feel awkward.

Every year, every single year
I seem to need that phantom reminder
of how simple joy is
and how much happiness I can share,
just by opening my hand,
my heart, my mouth,
and tapping my two left feet.

Scrooge is reminded of choosing business success over love

The Ghost of Christmas (Priorities) Past,
shows me myself baking cookies at night
because doing it with kids
would take too much time,
also, picking a tree, making ornaments.

I see myself not-playing dreidel
with a Jewish friend,
not-reading that Christmas cozy mystery,
not-walking in the snow
with my dearest love …
eliminating
from my Christmas card list
those who did not write last year,
without wondering
what happened in their lives.

And so, this Spirit's visit to the heart
rattles the chains of past mistakes,
so I can arrive this time
alert, aware,
open to sweet, transitory joys
while I can still say, "I have not missed it."

The Ghost of Christmas Past leaves Scrooge

The jacob marleys we glimpse
on our own door knockers –
the honest knowing of family brokenness,
community dysfunction, church mistakes,
the isolations of the pandemic,
and the cultural past
of intolerance, racism and violence –

mixed up with holy long ago,
and remembered in jumbled fashion

are seen in crèche, sung in carol,
written in scripture,
and re-written in poem, story,
film, pageant –

and somehow, we become gentle
with those around us who are visited
by their own Christmas ghosts.

Ebenezer is taken by the Ghost of Christmas Present to witness the unexpectedly happy Christmas of people Scrooge considers unfortunate.

In cratchit chrismases everywhere.
people choose joy,
though I assume they should be miserable.

Carols are sung
in a home with hospice
and gifts exchanged at a homeless shelter –
exchanged not "given-out."

Visits are skyped with soldiers deployed,
and thin bright tinsel-smiles
pass between parents
holding their babies in NICU.

This year there is
a virtual stream of memorials,
and yet deep-as-santa laughter
in a memory care unit,
a drug rehab,
a fire evacuation center,
the self-quarantine of COVID-19,

and I notice we are blessed – everyone.

Scrooge observes the Christmas Day celebration of his nephew Fred whose invitation he turned down as a waste of time

My inventory of rejected invitations
includes a play
performed by rank amateurs,
a child's dance recital,
a pick-up basketball game,
a board game night,
and much good food and laughter,
I was too busy to enjoy.

I have it on the best authority,
that God right now is at a rent party,
swinging wildly at a piñata,
willing to be foolish,
acting out Christmas carol charades,

in fact pantomiming
all twelve verses of that pear tree song,
swapping cookies, stacking poinsettias,
celebrating chosen families,

while I earnestly do a job, clean a house ... even
take volunteering or wrapping too seriously.

Scrooge is shown two hidden children, Want and Ignorance. "Beware them," says Christmas, "beware Ignorance the most."

Every hungry child is mine.
Every homeless child is mine.
Every abused child,
every child
who has been made ignorant,
full of hurt, full of anger – is mine.

The murdered child
and the child who murders are mine.

There is no hiding
behind the manger or the sleigh.

More than food basket,
toy drive, heating oil for winter,
dresses for the prom …
more than one well dug,
school built, shipment of vaccine,
free dental care or virtual therapy,
and yet including them all,
this one thing is true.

At the intersection of want and ignorance
is Bethlehem.

The Ghost of Christmas Yet to Come shows Scrooge the death of Tiny Tim, possible if there is no intervention

The pointing finger writes
warnings on walls,
forgiveness in the dust,
and hope in the trajectory of a star.

but it always rests on a child –
a child in a manger,
a child with a crutch,
a child who is bullied, hungry, hurt,

a child who flees to safety
and wants to wake up
in a home and with love.

Then the finger points
at those who could help, but don't.

Scrooge is shown a pawn shop selling the sheets and curtains of his bed and his clothes

God, it's not the sheets and blankets
of the bed I've been lying in –

but stripped and for sale
is the fabric of the earth –
and the curtains of the polluted sky.

The fish are my business,
and birds of the air that will sing
or will be silent
because of what I do.
The climate is my business,
the health of those who have no bubble
is my business,

And keeping Christmas all year long
is swaddling
all God chose and chooses still.

The Ghost of Christmas Yet to Come offers another chance to ... curmudgeons

This draped and ominous ghost,
of Christmas yet to come
is one of my favorite fictions,
for it comes to me, saying – it's not too late!

It came to old people
who messed up most of their chances,
un-wise men and women,
on long journeys with weird gifts,
menopausal Elizabeth,
angel-got-your-tongue Zach,
always in the way, Simeon,
Anna, a biblical example of dementia,

grumpy, greedy, grim,
grasping, grinchy Scrooge ... and me.

We are invited to change –
hang out windows to buy turkeys
for people who only need a loaf of bread,
go to dance parties
with taps on our walkers,
give to the poor,
shelter the vulnerable,
raise salaries for essential jobs,

unsay what we have said,
try to undo all the harm past,
laugh and laugh,
never minding who laughs at us,

and find a source of Christmas joy
so deep and wide and true
it lasts all the days,
all our few-left precious years.

The best-known line in "A Christmas Carol" is spoken by Tiny Tim

God, you find the Tiny Tim
inside of everyone –
both brokenness and courage.

We are absolutely fragile
and marvelously strong,
each needing a circle of love –
a corner by the fire, a friend or family –

but, also the unexpected
intervention of compassion.

And, from both the deep night
and the brightest gift,
you call forth
the shocking
universality of benediction –

God bless us, everyone.

"He went to church and walked about
the streets and watched the people
hurrying to and fro ... and found he
took pleasure in it all."
A Christmas Carol

I haven't missed it –
the listening to Luke's stories,

fruitcake and wrapping presents,
the lighting of candles,
giving a waitperson a stunning tip,
stuffing the bell-ringers kettle,
really, even knowing it's not enough,
making amends
on the debts of my heart.

I'll party with anyone who asks –
even my relations,
visit a friend who doesn't expect me,
greet a stranger on the street
through my mask,
who long may have given up
expecting anything.

I haven't missed it –
and now I can live a little in the past
and the present and the future,
balanced on love.

I will keep Christmas well –
March and June and gold October, too,
even Advent,
when it comes again.

Some Poems
from Traditions
... Old or Newer

A Conversation
about Her

I tell my friend
that I visit the Black Madonna
almost every day in advent,
a digital pilgrimage,
praying
at shrines in Detroit, Atlanta, Houston,
at our Lady, Mother of Ferguson
and all those killed by gun violence.

I look for new art, often graffiti,
T-shirts, Etsy prints, ink,
ancient icons of her
written all over the world,
and her many statues in chapels
are knee-deep in old miracles, new tears.

My friend asks – Do I gaze
at the Black Madonna
to understand white privilege?

No, I get that
from pretty much all the other images.

Is it to become anti-racist?
I know which book she's read.

True. Yes. That. This year.

I resist saying – it's not my first year,
because that would be
just one more white person strategy
to prove I'm more activist than you.

However, I do not completely resist
congratulating myself.

I want to be clever,
and say I visit the Black Madonna to pray –
what could be more natural?

Also true. Also betraying
white love of power-steering.

My friend's skin is more like mine,
(fewer wrinkles) than like Mary's,
so why not be honest
and tell her why
I really need this contemplation?

I go to the Shrine of the Black Madonna,
and I don't understand her,

but, when I go,
I know she understands me.

Las Posadas

There is always a knocking on doors
that exposes the unwelcome
of the heart
for those who are different, poor,
those who don't have
reservations
in a particular motel of the mind.

So there is a turning away
of immigrant, transgender, Black,
of indigenous people
who are the here-before
to what grabs the power-now.

Yet they all camp in the backyard
and have a party.

For the God of Las Posadas,
says always, "here I am,
the baby, the piñata – break me."

Mistletoe

Basket on high
is the translation from the Navajo
of a parasite
that makes nests
for spotted owls and diamond firetails
and causes juniper berries to grow.

It feeds all forest creatures,
and invites kisses.

It must have been hanging nearby
when Joseph whispered,
"you know I love you anyway,"
and she replied, "... but do you trust me?"

and he paused, sucking in
a great gulp of the mystery,
and kissed her

and the kiss was sweeter to Mary
at that moment
than a skyful of angels.

Fields and floods, rocks, hills and plains ...

God of the backyard tree
and the beach at the end of the subway line,
arroyo, pine forest, orange grove,
the protected kauri, the national park,
zen sand garden in a nursing home,

the constellations,
and, in places where stars cannot be seen,
moonrise through windshield,
hospital window, bars.

We are blessed by places in nature
where we find peace.

Remind us, Dirty God,
to seek them out
when life comes unraveled.

And, to be fair,
we pray for creation as well –
victim of the violence
of climate change and pollution,
the waste of resources,
poisoning of air, water, land,
mountain-top removal coal mining,
fracking, rainforest clearing,
melting of ice caps,
and exhaustion of arable soil.

Remind us, Warming God,
not to stop at pray,
but vote, boycott, write,
call, carry a sign,
tie one wrist to a chain link fence,
spend some money or time in jail –

that heaven and nature,
nature, nature, nature, nature – sing.

Magnificat

And Mary – the Mary who always
appears when she is needed

turquoise, stars and blooming roses,
to Mexican children
or the dementia clairvoyance of the old,
now and in the hour of their death.

This Mary says to her cousin,
Elizabeth, big and swollen-ankled with
her menopausal maternity,

"My soul is a lens for God,
my spirit castanets,
for God has made me pregnant
for the sake of all children forever,
the Mighty One finds sanctuary
in my human lactation.

God brings health care justice to all
and denies the wealthy the power of prescription;
gives clean wells to Africa
and takes away designer water bottles;
calls bans of blessing
on men who love men and women who love women,
and calls transgender – "Born again."

God deploys these new forces –
hope for the suicidal,
peace for the undocumented immigrant,
joy for the jobless,
love for those whose lives
have been twisted by incest …

remembering the fertility of Eden,
promise of Ararat, repentance of Nineveh,
Isaiah's holy mountain menagerie,
and the cross and alleluia
curled fetal even now
beneath this frail diaphragm
that breathes in one young woman a song.

Lighting the Dark

There is a kindness in lights.

Some houses display window candles
or a decorated tree,
others have bushes and trees
festooned with twinkling nets,

Others electrify a piece of story
in white-wire reindeer,
nibbling the yard,
sleigh or star on the roof,
inflated characters –
Grinch, Scrooge and Santa,
Snoopy, Lucy, Frosty,
a full plastic crèche with a manger
and a camel, also angels,
and, of course, Rudolph.

The sophisticated find this tacky,
but sometimes I need faith
really bright,
public and of questionable decorum –
a multitude of the LED host,
like it was so long ago.

Then, when I walk in the night,
I can find my way –
for I always have miles,
miles and miles to go before I sleep.

The Johannine Nativity

In the beginning was the Word
and the Word was with God
and the Word was love, or light, or create-this.
In the beginning was the Word
and the Word was Hail and Mary,
manger, jingle, star.
In the beginning was the Word
and it was Qur'an and Ganesh, Yahweh, Tao.
And the Tao was with God and
in the manger was God.
The Hail to a young girl was with the create-this.
All that came into being was Allah,
and the light shone on the Ganges
and there were bodhisattvas
who were not afraid.

In the beginning was the Word,
who let us write it.
The Qur'an was written on the darkness
and the darkness became a Star.
Many men and women were sent from God,
with very many names,
and they pointed and chanted,
burned sage, whirled, sweat,
fasted and prophesied to the love
so that all would believe.
They were words, not the Word,
but they spoke without fear.

The manger child with the crossed-heart
comes into the world
and there is a turning away –
the jealous claiming of the Word
that ends up spitting it out.

But where there is a turning toward,
the listening straw meets the children of God
who are born …
not so much in their own traditions,
as on the articulating breath of God.

Word becomes flesh – dangerous
and so very often divisive
but hope lives among us
and we speak and write its glory,
as long as we do not pretend to understand.

Improv on Dr. Seuss'
The Grinch who Stole Christmas

(a parody)

The grinch on the inside of who you and who me
who shrinks from the carols and ducks under the tree ...

The grinch who fears weight gain and avoids every store,
with chestnut-roast muzak and wreaths on the door ...

The grinch who dreads greedies and commercials for toys,
and deplores the way sadness is wrapped in fake joy ...

This grinch has a heart that is just the right size,
but it hurts so at Christmas that it is no surprise ...

That with all of the darkness, the hurry, the haste,
with all of the "must-do's," the parties and waste ...

The grinch on the inside of you-grouch and me-beast,
the grinch who hates candlelight service and feast ...

The grinch who is lonely, and feels like a stranger,
the grinch who's disgusted when I rhyme with "manger" ...

Finds that all of the stories of this Christmas season,
the Scrooges and Nutcrackers point to one reason.

It's a Wonderful Life, White Christmas, Fred Claus,
and the Polar Express are all written because –

There's a mystery here, there's a wonder, a glow,
that comes not from a package or starlight on snow ...

That is not about family with its comfort or grief,
and is not about having some perfect belief ...

It's all about God, who won't come the right way.
who jumps out of the church, as well as the sleigh …

God who needs diapers but takes myrrh in a pinch –
this God who sends babies is in love … with each Grinch.

The Long O
of Advent

O Antiphons are used at Vespers of the last seven days of Advent in several Christian traditions. They are referred to as the "O Antiphons" because each one begins with "O" and a metaphor / parable name of Christ and they call upon Christ to come.

The traditional list is O Wisdom, O Adonai, O Root of Jesse, O Key of David, O Dayspring, O Monarch of Nations, O Emmanuel, which means God-with-us.

O parable-maker,
Christ

O Gambler on hope, O Beggar of peace,
O Clown of joy,
O you who are pulled out of line
by the homeland security of every country
every faith, every self-satisfaction,
every intolerance,
because you cross our boundaries
with concealed love …
come and teach us how
to be advent people.

O antiphon for those who wait

Come, O Word, to our waiting

come to the emergency room,
come, to job interview, cancelled flight,
and the restaurant table
with two menus,
and only one chair filled.

Come, to the hospice bed
and those who sit around it,
to the inbox of a high school senior
hoping for early decision
and the courtroom
before the jury returns,
to the swelling under the heart
of those in their third trimester,
the phone-watching
of anyone for test results,

and, late-night cardoor-bang listening
of those who expect
an adolescent to return home.

You, who come to our beginnings
and to our endings,
also breathe a sweet blessing
on the hard pauses
life gives along the way. amen

O antiphon for those who suffer sexual violence

O Adonai, of the hidden name,

hold tenderly in your love,
those who cannot
bear a kiss,
those who have asked for a fish
and been given a snake,

children, women, men –
raped, trafficked, abused,
those who suffer from incest,
unwanted touching,
cyber shaming, date rape,
those harmed or disbelieved
into silence
those threatened for secrets,
heart-sick mute.

Wrap them in the least invasive
come-unto-me,
and teach us to offer them always
a cup of cool listening. amen.

O antiphon for Advent
in the Pandemic

O come, our Shelter-in-Place,
be a manger for everyone.

O come, Essential Word,
worker of creation in the beginning,
now in the prison,
the hospital or nursing home,
grocery store, delivery truck,
meatpacking plant –

come and rub temples,
and smooth tears from the cheeks
or those who are trying so hard
not to touch their own faces.

O come, zooming hope.
O come, bear-in-the-window tenderness.
O come, graduation parade joy.

O come, pan-lover of us all –
come to Wuhan province,
to Italy, to London, to Haiti,
to New York City, Florida,
Texas, India, Brazil,
and to places
that never made the news.

Come to the saging ones,
holding their last gift of myrrh,
to the children
with pediatric multi-symptom
inflammatory syndrome,

come to those who grieve
friends, family,

a small business or a wonderful job,
a home, a fragile mental balance,
trust in the future.

Come to Black people in America,
suffering a disease
spread by particles of injustice,
for year after year after year,
Covid-1619.

Come with incarnation,
come as Emmanuel.
Remind us where you truly are.

O antiphon for the Festival of St. Nicholas
(December 6 or December 19)

O Ho-Ho-Ho-sanna, O Giver of gifts,
O Saint-maker of us all,

Nick our hearts
that we may bring bread to the hungry,
protect children when their hope is stolen,
open up the casks of well-hidden crimes,
still storms and raise the dead,

that we may toss handfuls
of unexpected joy
into the empty shoes and drying socks
of sleeping neighbors,

and by horse or by donkey,
on a sleigh or a ship,
in a polar express or a 34th street miracle –

share love with all the world.

O antiphon for those
in recovery

O come, One Dayspring at a time,
to those with a white chip
or the bronze of thirty years,
going forward together
into the drinking holidays.
Come and give us serenity.

Come to the dual diagnosed,
in the meeting room
with the dark of solstice all around,
loneliness and loss,
and an illness for which steps
may be too simple.
Come and give us courage.

Come to those whose bottom
took away family,
and whose recovery
takes away barroom friends.

Come to many, especially women,
for whom "powerlessness"
sticks in the throat.
Come and give us wisdom.

Come Higher Power
to those who put first things first
and those who put them last.
Come to those who need
to let go to let you,
and those who need to hold on
to be themselves.
Come to those off the wagon

and those running after it,
fingers desperately reaching.

Come to the sponsor
tired of calls in the night,
and the partner
wondering what defines – "enable."

Come to the state liquor store,
the county lock-up,
and the candlelight service.

Come with the miracle
that is – making a difference.

O antiphon for
all the beasts

O Hen, Eagle, Lamb, Dove, Aslan,
come for all friendly beasts –

for dogs who walk a shelter's perimeter
longing for a forever home,
also kittens, old cats, rats,
cockatiels, hamsters, rabbits,
ferrets, guinea pigs
and the Vietnamese potbellied pig ...

and for those you mourn –
seaside sparrow, passenger pigeon,
Javan tiger, dromedary, forest turtle,
mountain gorilla,
giant panda, snow leopard ...

Come as well for those on loan
to live nativities
from barnyards and 4H projects,

and the ones waiting for us
when we come home.

O antiphon for
the winter solstice

Come, O Darkness,
after the angels put out the stars,
Come, O baby who cried ...
for those who left, not just church,
but even the mall-version of this holiday
so far behind.

Come on the really slow polar local
for those who don't think
they have ever heard the bell.

Come to those who roll over,
putting pillows over their heads
when jacob marley's chains rattle
and those who went out to pee
just when Linus told everyone else
the meaning of Christmas.

Come to those with hearts
two sizes too small
because of all the terrible things
that happened to them –
some in the name of religion.

Come to those who go beyond SAD
to feeling like camel shit.

Come, and remind them
that when Mary was really cold,
she gave an angry kick
to the frankincense jar
(flashy gift but ultimately useless)
and then she saw it –

"Look what the magi really left us!
I can start this fire with
what fell behind the caravan's two-toed feet.

"Sometimes that's the only way
to warm a child of God."

O Tannenbaum

I will put in the wilderness the cedar, the acacia, the myrtle, and the olive; I will set in the desert the cypress, the plane and the pine together, so that all may see and know, all may consider and understand, that the hand of God has done this ... Isaiah 41:19-20a

O Tannenbaum,
rooted in ancient faiths,
hung with memories
of our children's childhoods,
or the popcorn,
glitter pine cones, and paper chains
of new families, blended families,
chosen families,
with brave new traditions.

O Charlie Brown trees,
sad trees –
already out on the sidewalk,
never picked at the lot,
left in the box in the attic
or still in the stand in March.

O Nutcracker-magic trees,
happy trees –
with branches of all earth's people,
shoot of Jesse tree,
planted by the streams of water,
standing in a field, clapping hands ...

and tree that will fall in a forest
and no one hear it –
that Christmas tree, too, that you know
because you know them all,

because you know us all –
how lovely, how lovely are the branches.

O antiphon for
Christmas Eve

O Emmanuel, born in the antiphony
between a Star
and a real umbilical cord,
between ho-ho-ho and humbug,
between our dreams for the perfect
candlelight service,
cantata, Christmas morning,
and a corny sitcom holiday special.

Come as our impossible hope,
come as a trivialized baby,
come anyway –

you who have always been willing
to be found in spilled wax,
and crumpled wrapping paper ...

Come.

Prayers from Songs of the Season

"I have no gift to bring -
Pa rum pum pum pum."
"Little Drummer Boy," Katherine Kennicott Davis

God, I come with my body –
hands in the gingerbread
with grandma-infused
muscle memory,
arms reaching an ornament
to the branch where it always hangs,

mostly my feeling-giftless-fingers
drumming on anything –

me and my coffee can, oatmeal box,
desk, sink, steering wheel, pew.
The dog and cat keep time
pa rum pum pum pum …

and you smile at me. amen

"Do you see what I see? A star, a star, dancing in the night, with a tail as big as a kite?"
"Do You Hear what I Hear?" Noel Regney and Gloria Shayne

God, we thank you Christmas
once came in hearing and seeing,
but also in the feel of the night wind,
the smell of stable straw
and frankincense –

God, we thank you that Christmas
comes alive
through the extravagant gifts

of people who do not see starlight,
but can explain it to a child,
of those who do not hear
a voice as big as the sea,
but understand what heart-song means,

of those who know in different ways,
like the unconditional kindness
often found among people
with Down syndrome,
the quick perception and sustained focus
now attributed to autism spectrum
and long ago to angels,

and those whose specific memories
limited by dementias,
let them pray for peace everywhere,
and for everyone.

*(Dedicated to my mother who could not see for the
last fifteen years of her vibrant living.)*

"Lord it's like a hard candy Christmas, I'm barely getting through tomorrow but still I won't let sorrow get me way down."
"Hard Candy Christmas," Carol Hall

God, the Savior comes even for folks
who make hard-candy Christmas
for others –
the murder inmate who was guilty,
the "at-fault" partner in a divorce,
pushers of fentanyl, perpetrators of incest,
protectors of sexual abusers
in faith contexts,
online bullies of teenagers,

and the leaders of nations
who abandon allies
and vulnerable populations,
who build walls, encourage misogyny,
shut down the government,
unbalance the peace of the world.

God, the Savior comes
for everyone –
but the angels announce it
to the ones barely getting through
tomorrow.

And so, Holy One, for those inside
a hard-candy Christmas

and even the ones
who make it that way,
as if that were just fine and dandy –

you offer a candy cane,
always a shepherd's crook, always hope.

*(This song from "Best Little Whorehouse in Texas,"
a Broadway musical and a film, was my daughter's
favorite Christmas tune when she was in elementary
and middle school.)*

"… Jesus the Savior did come for to die for poor orn'ry people like you and like I…"

"I wonder as I wander" John Jacob Niles, folk song collector, gathered from Annie Morgan in Murphy, North Carolina

God, you could call for a star,
speak a bird's wisdom,
conduct the philharmonic angels,

and yet you have come
for ordinary people –
the ones who are running away from you
just as fast as they can run,
the ones who don't want to look in the mirror,

Annie Morgan in her dirty dress,
singing her fragment of song seven times
each to earn a quarter,
Niles who wanted to collect the songs
of people who might never write,

my daddy whose family made moonshine
near where they met,
and sang the song aloud every year,
arms wore out from carrying
the tune in a bucket,
and the contralto soloist who knows
the beauty of holding every note,

one who performs salah five times a day,
a faithful Buddhist, a Jain,

all of us –
children with ordinary lives
and the very small songs,
you are collecting in your wide open love.

"Over the hills and everywhere"
"Go Tell It on the Mountain"
African-American spiritual song circa 1865,
compiled by John Wesley Work, Jr.

I am going to tell it on the mountain,
and at the border wall,
in city street and grocery aisle,
in shelter and courtroom,
board room and bar.

I am going to tell it
anonymously at the meeting
in the basement,
and climbing the old pulpit
where it has been heard
so many times before.

I am going to promise it
in a high school
where a student is wondering
whether someone has a gun,
dance it at a Quinceañera,
smile it in a memory loss unit
post it on social media
and whisper in a child's ear —

that Jesus Christ is born!

And It Comes...

'Twas the (ordinary) Cold Before Christmas

'T was the cold before Christmas and all through the church,
disinfectant I wiped, and, tissues, I searched.
The sermon I wrote was short as a wick
and that clamp laryngitis made my vocal cords thick.

My throat was on fire; my cough, it was croupy,
my nose red like a reindeer, but moist as a puppy.
All my Kleenex was crumpled, my lozenges shiny,
my headache was pounding, my eyes, they felt briny.

I went home to wrap presents and my smile – it was pasted,
but my family knew that I really was wasted.
So they sent me to bed with a bottle of pills,
socks for my feet, a space heater for chills.

And all Christmas Day, they made breakfast, played games,
drove the grandmothers home, till I finally exclaimed –
"I'm the mother. I'm needed. I'm in charge of this feast!
Without me it won't happen. No, not in the least!"

I struggled to stand, to my plans gave a whistle,
but they all flew away like … Clement Moore's thistle.
I sorted used ribbon in spite of frustration,
but a nap it enveloped my brave desperation.

So, defeated in bed, 'twas a whisper I heard,
"Christmas," it said, "doesn't come with your words."
The angel continued (I could just see the wings)
"Christmas, you know, doesn't mean you can sing.

"Christmas has come to the ill and the sneezing,
Christmas has come to the cranky or pleasing.
To the old and the young, to rich, middling and poor,
To the sad, it's a comfort, to the drowning, a shore.

"Christmas has come in spite of your plans,
or the fact that your plans are in other folks' hands.
Christmas has come by the child and the light.
So laugh at yourself, blow your nose and good night."

God, I didn't get it all done

I didn't get it ALL done.

I need to push. I need to push!
I need to PUSH!

And you say to me – "breathe,
just breathe, just breathe.

Now push.

It's too early; I'm not ready!

Yes, you are. Now push,
now breathe, push,
puff, puff, puff, push hard!

breathe, a little push, breathe.
Congratulations!"

and you lay a naked Christmas Day
on my belly.

For Twelve Days

Mourning after,
Tamir Rice

Go out today and find a child
with a toy in her hands,
with a toy at his feet, in his mouth,
find a child with a rattle
or puzzle, doll, matchbox, superhero.

It shouldn't be hard
so soon after Christmas.

Maybe you will see a child you love,
or one you've not met,
a kid from the neighborhood,
church, grocery store, NICU.

Look at this child
and pray for those who loved,
those who still love,
and all of those who will never
get a chance to meet
Tamir Rice, child with a toy.

Shall yourselves find blessing

I am swimming in the first light
the day after Christmas,
slowly with my torn meniscus
but more quickly than
the woman who comes in,
with a bright yellow swimsuit
and a cane
and asks to share my lane
for her walking.

She says, "Merry Christmas,"
I reply, "and a Happy Boxing Day."

The next time we turn
face to face at the same end
at the same time,
she says, "Feast of St. Stephen …"

And I start to walk and sing,
"Good King Wenceslas looked out
on the feast of Stephen,
when the snow lay round about
deep and crisp and even …"

And she joins me and we sing together,
walking in the same direction.

"Brightly shone the moon that night
though the frost was cruel
when a poor one came in sight
gath'ring winter fuel."

And then we keep on singing –
two old women,
both injured and slow,
walking in each other's
wet footsteps
the day after this Christmas
with its rare full moon –

about compassion
and how it always follows
the feast of the birth of God.

Tinsel

The legend tells of a holy family
fleeing the violence against children
Herod brought to Bethlehem.

Weary to the point of exhaustion,
they went into a cave and fell asleep
on the long road to Egypt.
A kind spider, who could think
of no other gift,
wove a web
across the mouth of the cave
and, when the soldiers came to kill them,
they saw the web gleaming
with the morning dew
and assumed no one was inside.

We remember the spider
by hanging tinsel on Christmas trees,
and we remember
that strands insubstantial as cobweb
still keep our children safe.

Our thin and easily broken web
of words and deeds
for children in poverty,
children trafficked as slaves
or sex workers, refugee children,
indigenous girls,
children fearful
of those who should love them,
make just safe-enough caves
and sweet places for resting.

The story of violence long ago
was not of one family so special
they were protected
when other children died,
but that all the cruelty of the world
is challenged by spun thread,
and one child saved
is a promise
to every child who lives in fear,
to all the weeping parents.

New Year's Eve Morning

Pink dawn fingers the grey bark
on the maple trees
along the frost-heaved stone wall
and I see it through the kitchen window.

Next to the window hangs
a calendar already turned to January,
although we haven't yet lived
the last day of the old year.

(So eager we are to be done with it.)

The calendar boasts a picture
of a hunting beagle.
Our beagle is sleeping on the sofa,
also a picture ... of entitlement.

In the frame of the window
beyond the trees
but not yet touched by light,
I see the parked truck of our neighbor
who nearly died last winter
of heart disease.

Old wall, old sun
new page –
we have them every day.

A New Year
and a Small Cow

My youngest grandson
chooses an animal from the crèche,
different every time –
walking around with a cow
tight in his small hand,
or a sheep, a donkey, a dove,
the camel with the funny expression.

He holds them up for us to see,
then turns and pets the dog
who follows him
because he is a reliable source
of much scattered food.

I watch him – determined,
but a little unsteady
on his course around the house,
and I am reminded –

the beasts are friendly,
and the children will lead us.

I am packing up pieces of Christmas
as we turn to New Year,
wondering –
what I will need to hold tightly
from this story
on my small path through the days
till advent comes again?

Epiphany, the story comes again...

There's the story about the pregnant woman
whose fiancé married her anyway
and how they traveled together
to the crowded city
where an innkeeper offered a stable,
and the animals shared a hospitality of hay.
And there's the sequel about shepherds
who were watching their flocks by night,
all seated on the ground
when the angels came harmonizing
SATB in the sky
and sent them to Bethlehem
to see the child born for them
and then to share those good, good tidings.

And that's what they did —
they went back to the fields all christmasy,
greeting everybody
with good will, peace on earth ...
though probably not chestnuts.

But then there's the other plot line
that gets folded into the bathrobe pageant
though it happened weeks
or even years later —
about the travelers and their gifts
and the detour home
to avoid the homicidal Herod.

And that's what makes us part of the story –
not because we are wise and
certainly not royal,
but because we're always late or lost,
and, if we arrive at the holiness of it at all,

we come with road dust on our feet,
and star dust in our hair.

epiphany story

"I wanted a bride doll,"
the church musician said,
when I asked him
about Christmas gifts
in his childhood.

"And the sadness is –
that it came a year too late,
while my parents agonized
over their little boy
who asked Santa
for such a scary toy,

but the joy is –
that the second Christmas
my mother handmade
every satin ruffle,
each trim of lace –
there was so much love
in that doll,
it was fit for a manger."

Sometimes it takes
a long journey, trusting
a very distant star
to be wise enough

to leave the baseball bat
on the shelf,
and give the frankincense.

According to Matthew

The star stopped,
over the place where the child lay.

But anyone who ever observed
a star at its rising
knows better –
knows foot-blistered, homesick,
camel-groin-sore,
searching the night sky ... better.

The star always proceeds,
until the wise
save ice caps, rainforests, and islands,
heal dementia, welcome refugees,
find missing indigenous women,

until those with the power
are disin-heroded,
and enter the house of justice,

until the magi
bring magic gifts to the world –

in symphony and street art,
music and movies,
youtube, zentangle, samba and slam.

The star stops only long enough
for everyone to find
a place to set their presents down,

dream, take another road.

I'll keep it there

The glass magi was separated
from the other figures of the crèche –
as magi always are
by time and by their origin
as strangers,
perhaps language, hijab
(for who knows the gender anyway),

deep wrinkles around the eyes,
from looking so long into the desert
and searching the sky for a star.

And perhaps by loneliness –
no one really wants
to go home another way.

The unboxed magi
teeters next to an aloe plant
and a small bowl of garlic bulbs
on the window sill
above the sink
and all my fragile dirty dishes.

It reminds me the journey
out of this season
will not be about fear
of some elf on the shelf
who watches, calculating
the good and bad
in my life,
and worthiness for presents,

but rather a touchstone,
or touchglass,
when I need to remember
I am one of the givers

to this precious
and most vulnerable child,
who is, after all,
as ordinary as
a bowl to be broken.

And What
Comes Next...

For this Time Being
(After W.H. Auden)

Well, so this is that again.
We are still dismantling trees,
unwinding lights
of yet another year's celebration,
packing our traditions in cardboard boxes
up to the attic, kissed with uncertainty
more Advent than Epiphany.

The children now are adults –
they came for Christmas
but we gave them our best gifts years ago,
and we can no longer expect them
to follow our stars, only their own.

Our parents are children now
and we try hard for them to feel
a hint of wonder,
afraid each holiday will be their last.
We abandon visiting everyone,
at least the cousins, except on Zoom,
content with minimal active love
that lets them be odd or cantankerous –
less Currier and Ives,
more Modern Family.

As in previous years,
we experienced the Vision –
in a swish of a child in a monarch's robe,
the dry rustle of bed clothes
at a caroling visit,
a stocking smaller than store-bought
made by a great-aunt long dead,
the handmade gift of a first grader
kept secret by a prodigious act of will.

We have seen that Child but,
still be-Audened,
we have credit cards to pay off,
laptops and tablets to charge,
texts not so holy and posts and memes,
and all the selfies of Christmas
trivial against the good friday newsfeed
of Black men who cannot breathe.

It is a plain Time Being we share,
but it is still redeemed
both its hope and suffering, too,
by how the story is told.

And we will need to meet ordinary days,
that shelter-in-place
we call life,
with extraordinary courage,
each one a rehearsal for an Easter

in which a Spirit practices
across our keys the scales of joy.

About the Author

Maren C. Tirabassi is the author of twenty-one books, many published by The Pilgrim Press, including **A Child Laughs: Prayers of Justice and Hope, Gifts In Open Hands – More Resources for the Global Community**, and **Transgendering Faith**, which was nominated for a Lambda Award.

Maren's love for all things Christmas is obvious in her short story collection **The Shakespeare Reader and other Christmas Tales** which places the Bard's characters into seasonal plots. Holiday audio productions include *Sticky Mittens and Angel Feet* and *I Think I See a Star*.

In addition to receiving The Pilgrim Press Leadership Award, she served as Poet Laureate of Portsmouth, NH and was recently the Scholar in Residence at Vaughan Park Anglican Retreat Centre in Aotearoa New Zealand.

A graduate of Union Theological Seminary in New York and Harvard Divinity School, Maren has been a United Church of Christ pastor in Massachusetts and New Hampshire since 1980. She facilitates creative writing workshops in a range of settings from recovery group to senior center, correctional facility to English Language Learning class. She and her husband Don Tirabassi live with Willie the beagle in Portsmouth, NH.

Maren C. Tirabassi is online on Facebook and at the WordPress poetry and global worship blog https://giftsinopenhands.wordpress.com/

She welcomes inquiries about her books, workshops and presentations at mctirabassi@gmail.com